Abuse

The GOSPEL for REAL LIFE series

Abuse: Finding Hope in Christ
Anxiety: Anatomy and Cure
Borderline Personality: A Scriptural Perspective
Cutting: A Healing Response
God's Attributes: Rest for Life's Struggles
Vulnerability: Blessing in the Beatitudes

Brad Hambrick, Series Editor

Abuse

FINDING HOPE IN CHRIST

JOHN HENDERSON

P&R
PUBLISHING
P.O. BOX 817 • PHILLIPSBURG • NEW JERSEY 08865-0817

Library of Congress Cataloging-in-Publication Data

Henderson, John, 1974-
  Abuse : finding hope in Christ / John Henderson.
    p. cm. -- (The Gospel for real life)
  ISBN 978-1-59638-417-0 (pbk.)
  1. Adult child sexual abuse victims--Religious life. 2. Bible. O.T. Psalms XXII--Criticism, interpretation, etc. I. Title.
  BV4596.A25H46 2012
  248.8'6--dc23
                                      2012008774

I REMEMBER THE FIRST TIME Claude and Patricia walked through my door. It was a Tuesday. It was cold and raining. A swirl of pain, confusion, and anger entered the door alongside them. You could see it. You could feel it.

They had been married almost four years, none of them easy. The previous night had been especially difficult. In Claude's words, "it was our typical fight," beginning when he had initiated sexual intimacy and she recoiled. Claude had sighed and stomped away, feeling angry, rejected, and wronged. Patricia had retreated to a shell of bitterness and shame. While the minutes passed, Claude sat in their living room, wondering why he had married Patricia and why marriage to her was so disappointing. In their bedroom a few paces away, Patricia wondered why he demanded so much of her and had so little respect for her suffering.

The silence was broken by his accusations against her. He returned to the bedroom with a single question: "What's wrong with you?" The words cut deep. After a long pause, his other questions followed: "Why are you so selfish?" and "Don't you care about me or our marriage?" Patricia perceived no choice but to defend herself and offer a few accusations of her own: "Nothing is wrong with me . . . you're the problem . . . you don't care about me or what I have been through . . . you just want sex!" Her words cut deep, too. The situation escalated into shouting before Claude retreated to a spare bedroom for the night, slamming doors along the way.

The scene was not unfamiliar to them. It may be somewhat familiar to you, too, or to those you love. At first glance it just seemed like a big fight, but beneath the surface raged an ocean of shame, bitterness, and despair. There was a world of painful memories, confusion, and dishonor that they had never thought to bring before God and face together through the gospel of Jesus Christ.

The suffering that Patricia had experienced and to which she now felt enslaved was physical and sexual abuse from her childhood. According to Patricia, it was "always in the background of our marriage." Her experiences of abuse subtly influenced the way in which she saw God, herself, and her husband. She didn't like the realities of her past, but tried to live with them as best she could. Claude didn't like the realities of her past, either, and wanted them to fade away quietly. He wanted the past to stay in the past. Neither Claude nor Patricia thought God had anything profound or transformative to say about their situation.

GOOD NEWS IN A BROKEN WORLD

None of us can escape the brokenness of our world. We are sinful, hurting people surrounded by other sinful, hurting people in a universe groaning under the curse of sin. The reality of physical and sexual abuse in our world provides a blatant and painful proof of this brokenness. If we look and listen carefully, we see and hear of abuses and assaults everywhere. Some of us have experienced these horrors firsthand. Some of us know loved ones and dear friends who have suffered under cruelties unspeakable. What are we to think and do? What does the gospel have to say to us when we are victims of evil? How do we love and help men and women who have suffered under various forms of abuse?

I have wrestled with these questions for years. Perhaps you have as well. Abuse stirs up all kinds of questions: "How do I face and understand the abuses I have suffered in the past?" "Where was God, and why did he allow it?" "What am I to think of him . . . of myself . . . of the pain?" "Was it

God's will for me to be abused?" "Did my abuse grieve and anger him?" "By not stopping it, was he a part of it?" "How am I supposed to believe that God loves me if, according to his sovereign purpose, he ordained for me to be treated with such brutality?" I think the list of doubts and wonderings could go on for pages.

These are a few of the questions that we are interested in exploring throughout this booklet. In no way do I propose to have all the answers. I do believe, however, that God knows all the answers and has shared some of those answers with us. He has spoken to us in his Word. The answers that Scripture offers are not easy to digest, but they are available. God comforts the afflicted through his Word. The gospel speaks into our worst nightmares. The beauty and light of the gospel often shines most brilliantly through the darkest and most distressing surroundings. Present-day evils and afflictions can, by the grace of God, help us to taste and see the glory of Christ.

"He delivers the afflicted in their affliction, and opens their ear in time of oppression" (Job 36:15). The ways and words of the Lord do not always take the form we expect, but they always deliver at the proper time. The God of all grace opens our eyes and ears to see and hear whatever comfort and hope we require in the moments or seasons when we require them. I think we should be glad for this.

The stories, realities, and truths of the Scripture are often not very clean and tidy. I think we should be glad for this, too. After all, real life on earth can be very unclean and untidy. The lives unfolding in the pages of God's story can be brutally messy and deeply disturbing, just like our own. The world that God sees and documents in the Bible runs full of sin and strife, just like the world we live in today. He describes the realities of human life with rugged honesty. He refuses to make it tame. He helps us to see the world just the way it is.

Then he helps us to make sense of life through his Word. He may not give us all the answers, but he gives us enough right answers for clarity, fruitful life, and godliness to happen *over time*. The Scripture reveals who God is and how he operates in a universe of broken pieces. It shows us how he is putting it all together through his redeeming grace so that we may marvel and worship—he is putting it all back together through Jesus Christ:

> For it was the Father's good pleasure for all the fullness to dwell in Him, and through Him to reconcile all things to Himself, having made peace through the blood of His cross; through Him, I say, whether things on earth or things in heaven. (Col. 1:19–20)

My hope and prayer in writing will be to demonstrate how the Word of God speaks vividly to us amid and after severe abuse, and how the sovereign love and grace of God in Jesus Christ provide eternal, solid hope and incomprehensible comfort to the afflicted. We will look at one couple, one counseling meeting, and one psalm, praying that the Lord will grant us grace to behold the depth of his wisdom and love in order for us to live triumphantly in the wake of abuse.

THE LIFE PATRICIA HAD KNOWN

Patricia's story was long and painful. Words cannot really capture what she had experienced, nor how her life unfolded in the wake of abuse. An older brother molested her for several years, sneaking into her bedroom in the middle of the night, forcing her to touch him and shamelessly touching her, threatening to kill her pet rabbit if she ever told. All of this was before the age of eight. A maternal uncle molested her during his monthlong visit with her family and then raped her on the last night of his stay. Patricia was nine years old. The uncle left, and she never saw him again. Her mother "turned a blind eye." Her father was drunk and checked out. Her older brother knew about her rape, and laughed.

So Patricia kept it all to herself. During adolescence she felt attracted to older, proud, and popular boys. If they would give her a little attention, then she eagerly gave them her body. She bounced from boyfriend to boyfriend. It was not uncommon for Patricia to stay out all night. No one seemed to miss her at home. After waking up one morning in a stranger's house, naked, hung over, and seventeen years old, surrounded by other half-naked people passed out on the floor, Patricia felt hopeless and humiliated. At that point, she recalled, she wished for death.

By the grace of God, Patricia didn't take her life, but instead accepted an invitation to attend a church camp the following week. During that week she heard the gospel for the first time in her life. "The blood of Christ pays for your sins completely," she was told. She could be "forgiven, cleansed, and made a new creation in Christ." It was news too good to be true. The Spirit helped her to believe the news and trust in Christ for her salvation. Life slowly began to change. Older, godly women began to seek her out at church and spend time with her in the Scripture. Home remained a wreck, but she didn't really care anymore. Long-standing acquaintances began to snub and mock her, but she didn't mind at the time. This new hope in Christ was worth the cost.

Life went on, and Patricia exerted a lot of energy to leave her past behind. The shame, disgust, and rage that she had been feeling for many years, like a kind of cancer, "went into remission." She didn't talk about it with anyone. On her eighteenth birthday, she left home for good. By working hard at various jobs, Patricia could afford to live with a couple of friends and buy a car. Two years later, she met Claude. They fell in love, were engaged a year later, and married.

THE LIFE CLAUDE HAD KNOWN

Claude lived a different kind of childhood. He was an only child to a father retired from the armed forces and a mother who made sure that Claude suffered as little as possible. It was a Christian home, but full of anxiety and legalistic standards. "If something was wrong," he believed, "I fixed it, because that is what you are supposed to do." He was a take-the-bull-by-the-horns sort of man, a high performer, and "never one to fall into self-pity." Committed to Christ from a young age, Claude knew the gospel and believed salvation comes through Jesus Christ alone by faith alone.

While Claude knew that Patricia had a tough past, including some sexual abuse, he had "expected her to be fine." Since their sexual encounters with each other were so easy and fun before marriage, he assumed that they would be even better after marriage. So when their honeymoon night arrived, and Patricia retreated from him in fear and terror, Claude was taken completely off guard. Not only was he humiliated, he was angry. All his attempts to fix his wife in the months to follow failed. He had always had the right answers. He hadn't done anything wrong. "What was her problem?"

THE GOD THEY AVOIDED

So now, in his marriage to Patricia, Claude didn't have a clue what to think or do. Neither did Patricia. A whirlwind of painful emotions, anger, and disappointments clouded their vision and hearing. Perhaps most striking was their total avoidance of God in their daily lives. Our early meetings together brought this into the open. They didn't talk to God in honest, personal ways. They struggled to listen to his Word in honest, personal ways. From their point of view, he couldn't really be trusted. Patricia experienced the Lord as being "ashamed of me," "aloof," and "uncaring." Claude saw God as wearing a perpetual frown, tapping his divine foot in displeasure, and waiting for them to "get our act together."

Both Claude and Patricia described Jesus Christ in distant, cold, and academic ways. They had great theological words, but no joy in him. They had good Bible answers, but little or no peace in Christ himself. Both Claude and Patricia could present the gospel point by point, but struggled to see any connection between the gospel and their marriage, or the gospel and their hardships, or the gospel and their sexual troubles.

In fact, both Claude and Patricia carried unconfessed, unacknowledged resentments and anger toward God. Recurring questions nagged them: "How could God have done this to me?" "How could he have allowed this to happen?" "Where were you, Lord?" "Why won't you let me out and give me help?"

This is the point at which Psalm 22 turned their world inside out, and for the better. They found in this single psalm words that captured their life before their eyes. They could see on the pages of Scripture their experience of life being described by God. They experienced firsthand the living and powerful Word of God, in which they were drawn into a conversation with their Father about their lives and his love, their pain and his grace. They began to know Christ and "the fellowship of His sufferings" (Phil. 3:10) with more clarity and hope. They could begin to see how God's redeeming love and grace comes freely to them in the very middle of abuse and pain, not simply to keep them from abuse and pain.

PSALM 22 IN THE WAKE OF ABUSE AND PAIN

It was a Thursday. We had been meeting for several months. Claude and Patricia seemed angry and discouraged. The question kept bouncing around: "Why is God refusing to help us or make all this better?" In the background behind that question was an even bigger question for Patricia: "Why did God let me be abused? Where was he? Why didn't he protect me? Why won't he protect me now?" We sought Psalm 22 for help—chewing on it a verse at a time. The first two verses seemed to capture their experiences in the moment as well as Patricia's experience of God over the course of her entire life:

> My God, my God, why have You forsaken me?
> Far from my deliverance are the words of my groaning.
> O my God, I cry by day, but You do not answer;
> And by night, but I have no rest.

When we read these words, we tend to think of Jesus Christ, and we should. He uttered these words on the cross (Matt. 27:46). The whole psalm points to Jesus Christ. But it also points to the painful realities of human life. While ultimately fulfilled in Jesus, the words were first expressed and absolutely experienced by David, and by all others who endure vicious affliction. In particular, Patricia had *lived* these words for years. She had felt forsaken by God.

"God claims to be a God of justice," she thought, "yet I have lived under injustice. God says he loves his children, yet I have been unloved and mistreated." The God who described himself in Scripture as near and loving seemed to be a thousand miles from her daily life and struggles. She thought of him as a compassionate Father who answers prayers. "So why didn't he answer my prayers and care about me?"

When I asked Patricia, "Have you ever talked this way to God?," she replied without hesitation, "Never!" I asked her why not, and again she replied without hesitation, "I didn't think I was allowed to talk this way to God!" It was an important statement. In all her pain and humiliation, Patricia had never really faced her God and talked to him honestly. She had always grappled with her problems herself, away from God. In her mind, it was best to clean up first and then come to her Creator and Savior. Whenever she felt abandoned by God, Patricia ran from him rather than to him. In her experiences of shame, Patricia hid her face from him in further shame.

These first two verses of Psalm 22 declared to Patricia: *Face God*, no matter what. It will always be an unnatural motion when dealing with our experiences of abuse and torment, yet completely essential. Talk to him! Be candid with him! Bring it to him! As his beloved children, we will never have a time in our lives when he does not welcome our sincere cries: "As for me, I said in my alarm, 'I am cut off from before Your eyes'; nevertheless You heard the voice of my supplications when I cried to You" (Ps. 31:22).

These verses could encourage Claude in a similar way. In the face of frequent rejections, snubs, and suspicions from his wife, he felt lost and forsaken. God was inviting him to humbly bring them before his throne. Just as importantly, these words could help him to remember how to comfort and encourage his bride. In the middle of her fear and shame, he could invite her *toward God* rather than add fear and shame of his own. He could initiate prayer. Rather than quickly accuse her, he could patiently intercede on her behalf.

> Yet You are holy,
> O You who are enthroned upon the praises of Israel.
> In You our fathers trusted;
> They trusted and You delivered them.
> To You they cried out and were delivered;
> In You they trusted and were not disappointed. (Ps. 22:3–5)

Facing God in our affliction, while essential, will never be enough to live fruitfully in the wake of abuse. We must also learn to **trust God** in our affliction, based on who he is and his faithfulness from ages past. He is holy. He is faithful. In reading the few verses above, Patricia had to wrestle with the reality that she was not the first to endure unspeakable hardship in life, nor would she be the last. She was not alone, but had joined great legions of saints called to trust the Lord under awful circumstances. He has always delivered at the proper time. He would deliver her, too.

Now, this beautiful idea should not dismiss the realities of abuse. Celebrating the faithfulness of God in ages past and our union with fellow saints in suffering does not mean that we are minimizing the experience of being victimized. Rather, we are maximizing the reality of our fellowship in a redeemed and eternal community. We are maximizing the comfort we can receive from knowing that God has always been the Savior of lowly, destitute, and mistreated people:

> And all these, having gained approval through their faith, did not receive what was promised, because God had provided something better for us, so that apart from us they would not be made perfect. (Heb. 11:39–40)

This truth could also provide a direction for Claude as a husband. In these troubled moments, Patricia probably didn't need reminders about just how poorly she was acting as a wife. She already knew that. Patricia needed reminders of the pure, gracious, and trustworthy nature of our God—as we all do. He was with and for her and Claude. He was in control and could be trusted beyond their imagination. Claude could help Patricia to hear just how deeply God loved her and how faithfully he delivers.

> But I am a worm and not a man,
> A reproach of men and despised by the people.

All who see me sneer at me;
They separate with the lip, they wag the head, saying,
"Commit yourself to the LORD; let Him deliver him;
Let Him rescue him, because He delights in him." (Ps. 22:6–8)

The impact of these words on Patricia's countenance, by the grace of God, was both astounding and unforgettable. At this point in our meeting, she began to weep. "I am a worm and not a man, a reproach of men and despised by the people"—she knew exactly what David was talking about. She knew he was not using these words to express humility, but disgrace. These words seem to capture the inhumanity of abuse, especially sexual abuse. They describe the waves of subhumanness that Patricia had swallowed through her entire life. Sexual abuse left her feeling like an animal—a dirty, ugly animal. The years of immorality and debauchery during her adolescence had solidified this identity.

Then add the brutal weight of mocking. Just as Jesus heard these words hurled on him while he hung on the cross (Matt. 27:43), so Patricia had heard the *spoken and unspoken words* of her brother, mother, and father (and even her own conscience) scorning, dismissing, and blaming her at the height of her affliction. "I'm sure this was my fault . . . I could have done something to stop this . . . I must have led them on in some way." She assumed that everyone else blamed her, too.

Patricia recalled a cruel note that her older brother had slipped under her cereal bowl during breakfast on the morning he learned about her rape. It contained only two words: "Ha! Ha!" Such scorn haunted her, prompting her to think, "I deserved all this." Sometimes she asked, "Why hasn't God helped me?" At other times: "Why should he? Look at me. I'm disgusting."

It was also important for Claude to hear his wife voicing and reflecting on these words. Listening to Patricia express the inner turmoil and shame that she had been living in for so many years helped Claude to see a little more depth and dimension to her battle. He began to perceive a battle that cannot be won in an evening, or with a simple sentence of assurance, or through a three-steps-to-getting-over-abuse strategy. The reality of Patricia's internal fight and the implications for their marriage, he began to realize, weren't going away by themselves, nor would they go away quickly, but would require the ongoing grace of God. In fact, during the days after this meeting, Claude shared sorrow with Patricia for his lack of compassion, patience, and humble prayer for her in the past.

The words of the psalm were not leading Claude and Patricia away from reality, but inviting them to *face reality* head-on. God inspired David to paint a picture of real life and real suffering. After all, God speaks to real life. It was vital for Claude and Patricia to see that God does not live in denial. He sees troubles. He understands evil in greater detail than anyone else. The words of God were leading Claude and Patricia toward God and toward the realities of human life. To this point the psalm was crying out to them, "Face your God! Trust your God! Face reality!"

> Yet You are He who brought me forth from the womb;
> You made me trust when upon my mother's breasts.
> Upon You I was cast from birth;
> You have been my God from my mother's womb.
>
> Be not far from me, for trouble is near;
> For there is none to help. (Ps. 22:9–11)

At the precise moment of need, Scripture provided comfort to the soul. These were the truths that Patricia needed to hear and believe more than anything else: "You are God's. You have always been God's. He has always been near. He will always be near. He has been holding you this whole time. He always will." She heard the Lord telling her, "No matter where you have been or how you look and feel, you are mine!" The words of Psalm 22 were forcing Claude and Patricia to **know to whom you belong.**

Abuse can feel enslaving. It can feel as though you are now possessed and owned by other people. In a way, this is exactly what tyrannical and violent people communicate to those they abuse: "I own you . . . I can do to you whatever I want . . . You are my possession." These words from Psalm 22 demolish this lie. They cry out, "God owns you, loves you, and will forever be near to you. No one else has any right to your soul but *him*!"

Even more, the Lord was asking Claude and Patricia to realize that his relentless presence and deep affection for them did not mean painless, abuse-free life on earth. While he was near, trouble would also be near. God's love and earthly agony were not mutually exclusive conditions in their lives, but intimate friends. They went together. The conditions did not need to be reconciled because, under God's sovereign design, they were not in conflict.

Like all of us, Claude and Patricia had assumed that God's care for them would preserve them from suffering, when in fact it was his love preserving them in the midst of suffering. God loves his children passionately. Nothing can separate us from his love. This truth will never change:

> For I am convinced that neither death, nor life, nor angels, nor principalities, nor things present, nor things to come, nor powers, nor height, nor depth, nor any other created thing, will be able to separate us from the love of God, which is in Christ Jesus our Lord. (Rom. 8:38–39)

> Many bulls have surrounded me;
> Strong bulls of Bashan have encircled me.

They open wide their mouth at me,
As a ravening and a roaring lion.
I am poured out like water,
And all my bones are out of joint;
My heart is like wax;
It is melted within me.
My strength is dried up like a potsherd,
And my tongue cleaves to my jaws;
And You lay me in the dust of death. (Ps. 22:12–15)

In these verses David supplies graphic portrayals of oppressors and the oppressed. His poetry creates incredibly vivid images of predators and their prey. We cannot escape his description of the terrible impact of oppression and abuse. In fact, the expression "my heart is like wax; it is melted within me" elicited an unexpected image from Patricia's memory. It took her back to those late nights when she was awakened by the sound of her bedroom door opening, knowing that her older brother was *encircling*, and her stomach would turn. She could feel her heart melting within her chest and her soul collapsing in terror. She felt totally helpless.

In reading David's words, Patricia just couldn't believe that such honest depictions were in the Bible. She was stirred to ***face her weakness and desperation***. These were aspects of human life and suffering that she had always denied and resented. Even now in their marriage, Claude and Patricia felt forlorn and helpless to make anything better, and they blamed each other. They blamed God. They had never come to accept and appreciate the truth: "We are weak, vulnerable, and in the hands of God. Life may be full of pain, but it is also full of God's love, and we can always be thankful."

This part of the counseling discussion was especially difficult for Claude. Weakness and desperation were human experiences that he avoided, denied, and even resented. He was a fixer. When things went wrong, he prided himself on making them right. But he couldn't fix his wife. He couldn't make his marriage right. He resented her struggles. He resented the inconvenient pain that they brought to his life. Now he was being asked to acknowledge his smallness and insignificance. Only the Lord could bring restoration and healing to Patricia's soul and their marriage. Only the Spirit of God could give Claude gracious words to speak and humble ears to hear. Only Christ could grant him the compassion and love that he needed to know and display.

At the same time, Claude realized how adversarial he had become in his wife's life. Rather than an advocate, he was often an accuser. Rather than speaking to her with the comforting words of the gospel, he had often growled and roared with anger. He wasn't an abuser, but it was hard for Patricia to tell him apart from the abusers of her past. Claude began asking himself, "Am I a melting influence in my wife's heart or a strengthening influence? Am I drawing her away from Jesus or toward him?" Though he was not the reason for the agonies of her past, was he compounding them in the present? What role was he going to assume in her story?

> For dogs have surrounded me;
> A band of evildoers has encompassed me;
> They pierced my hands and my feet.
> I can count all my bones.
> They look, they stare at me;
> They divide my garments among them,
> And for my clothing they cast lots. (Ps. 22:16–18)

These words were absolutely eye-opening and heart-piercing for Patricia. Never had she connected the dots between her abuse and the abuse of Jesus Christ. Yet she could not escape the imagery of these verses and how they point directly at Jesus Christ and his crucifixion. For the first time in her life, it became clear that Jesus had gone before her in abuse—even worse abuse than she had endured. Jesus had absorbed the very wrath of God on her behalf. He had suffered as a human being. "But if when you do what is right and suffer for it you patiently endure it, this finds favor with God. For you have been called for this purpose, since Christ also suffered for you, leaving you an example for you to follow in His steps" (1 Peter 2:20–21).

Never had Patricia seen herself as someone who tasted "the fellowship of His sufferings" (Phil. 3:10). It was a beautiful moment. As the psalmist's words really began to soak into their hearts, Claude and Patricia actually saw themselves in fellowship with Christ as never before. Jesus seemed far more like them than unlike them. He became in their hearts a real Person who genuinely identified with their lives. Suffering in Christ offered them deeper fellowship with Christ. They started to **behold Christ amid their affliction**.

In the moments to follow, Patricia voiced an interesting shift of perspective: "So God planned for his own Son to suffer beyond belief. I wonder if sometimes I think that I am better than he is or should have somehow gotten a better deal." These were difficult words to swallow. They are humbling words. Yet they are vital words, because they sum up the essence of Claude and Patricia's standoff with God and with each other. Claude and Patricia were trapped under the unfairness and rottenness of their circumstances, fighting for new surroundings rather than new hearts transformed by grace. They had become so consumed with everything lost in the past that they couldn't grasp the glory to be gained in the present.

Admitting self-centered pride in these moments did not mean that they were admitting fault for abuses they had endured. The abuse that Patricia had suffered was never her fault. Rather, they were acknowledging how self-centered their view of their own lives had been to this point. Suffering quietly tempted their souls to go inward and focus on themselves. The more they were hurt, the more they could justify dwelling on themselves, defending themselves, and mourning everything in life that wasn't the way it should have been.

Claude and Patricia started to realize the importance of seeing the bigger picture of what God was doing to redeem, transform, and help them for the sake of his glory and kingdom. They were realizing that following in the footsteps of Jesus Christ could involve abuse, and that *he* was worth it. It meant believing that his grace was sufficient and that gaining Christ for eternity was worth all the suffering in the world: "For I consider that the sufferings of this present time are not worthy to be compared with the glory that is to be revealed in us" (Rom. 8:18).

> But You, O LORD, be not far off;
> O You my help, hasten to my assistance.
> Deliver my soul from the sword,
> My only life from the power of the dog.
> Save me from the lion's mouth;
> From the horns of the wild oxen You answer me. (Ps. 22:19–21)

God is near, and he will deliver at the proper time. How difficult to believe are these words? These verses asked Claude and Patricia to **remember that deliverance is certain and _to God_**.

In all our pains and tribulations, our prayer could always begin with these words: "O Lord, be not far off!" The certainty that God is near to his children provides true peace to those who believe it. Trusting that he is near us and for us gives the only real and lasting comfort: "Even though I walk through the valley of the shadow of death, I fear no evil, *for You are with me*; Your rod and Your staff, they comfort me" (Ps. 23:4). A beloved child can be bold and brave to face trials and danger in the presence of his or her father *because* the father is near and can intervene at a moment's notice. David is trying to remind himself of the certain, fierce, and always perfectly timed intervention of his heavenly Father. In fact, David sat convinced that God would hear and help him: "From the horns of the wild oxen You answer me."

When we read these three verses together, Claude and Patricia began to think about God's deliverance from a different viewpoint. They began to see the deliverance that God promised as first being deliverance *to* and *in* him. It was not first deliverance *from* pain. Deliverance from all abuses and suffering would certainly come someday, but not yet. In the meantime, he promises to be close. Jesus promises to satisfy their souls (John 4:13–14). He will comfort. He will be their refuge. He will be a shelter amid the storm. He will not always prevent the storm.

> I will tell of Your name to my brethren;
> In the midst of the assembly I will praise You.
> You who fear the LORD, praise Him;
> All you descendants of Jacob, glorify Him,
> And stand in awe of Him, all you descendants of Israel.
> For He has not despised nor abhorred the affliction of the
>   afflicted;
> Nor has He hidden His face from him;
> But when he cried to Him for help, He heard.
>
> From You comes my praise in the great assembly;
> I shall pay my vows before those who fear Him.
> The afflicted will eat and be satisfied;
> Those who seek Him will praise the LORD.
> Let your heart live forever! (Ps. 22:22–26)

The shift of focus and tone in verse 22 seems almost bizarre. The words move from expressions of torment and misery to expressions of awe and praise toward God. How on earth can Claude and Patricia be expected to "praise Him . . . ; glorify Him, and stand in awe of Him" in light of their painful histories and marriage? It may be difficult for any of us to imagine, but this is exactly what the moment calls for.

While suffering calls for heartfelt cries and mourning, it also calls for heartfelt worship toward God. Do you remember when Job received news that all his children had perished and all his possessions had been stripped away? "Then Job arose and tore his robe and shaved his head, and he fell to the ground and worshiped" (Job 1:20). Only Spirit-wrought faith can evoke such a beautiful response. Only the gospel can bring forth this kind of worship in our hearts.

THE GOSPEL IS A STORY OF DELIVERANCE AND RESTORATION

Shortly after sin entered the world through Adam, pain and toil entered the world, too. Suffering exists because sin existed first. God ordained them both. Shame, humiliation, murder, rape, and every other kind or effect of evil flooded into human experience because the human race, in Adam, scorned and disobeyed God. Every fragment and taste of suffering in this life reminds us of our sinful collapse in Adam. It highlights the darkness of human depravity. It heightens our sense of need for a Savior. Even undeserved abuse highlights the slavery and brokenness of our world. It can help to set the stage for deliverance and restoration by the grace of God.

On the heels of Adam's transgression and fall, God promised salvation and a Savior (Gen. 3:15). God followed his promise with a gracious act of atonement. He shed the blood of an animal in Adam and Eve's place in order to cover them with the skin: "The Lord God made garments of skin for Adam and his wife, and clothed them" (Gen. 3:21). He stripped away their attempts to achieve a righteousness of their own (using fig leaves) in order to cover them with his own righteousness (through his means of covering, the skin of an animal). This remarkable act of sacrifice and atonement foreshadowed the coming Messiah, "the Lamb of God who takes away the sin of the world!" (John 1:29).

The gospel tells us that we deserve wrath and eternal punishment, but have been given salvation instead. The wrath and punishment fell on Jesus Christ: "But He was pierced through for our transgressions, He was crushed for our iniquities; the chastening for our well-being fell upon Him, and by His scourging we are healed" (Isa. 53:5). God loved us and saved us while we were at our worst: "While we were yet sinners, Christ died for us" (Rom. 5:8). Though we were orphans, he has made us children. Though we were enemies before, he has made us friends. Though we were estranged from him and hostile to him, the Father has reconciled us back to himself through the cross of Christ. The gospel tells us how the Lord looks with mercy upon our deepest afflictions and brings deliverance.

Every story of abuse and mistreatment, by the grace of God, can become a story of deliverance and restoration. The story of the Bible showcases the glory of our God and his grace in hearing and saving the afflicted. The story of Adam and Eve was a story of salvation. The rest of the Bible tells story after story of deliverance and restoration. "For while we were still helpless, at the right time Christ died for the ungodly" (Rom. 5:6).

The stories of individual lives today can provide a similar showcase, especially when those stories are interpreted through the lens of God's Word. Through the stories of the afflicted, God proves that *he has not despised or abhorred the affliction of the afflicted.* In response to desperate human cries, God displays his compassion and love for those in agony. "But when he cried to Him for help, He heard. . . . The afflicted will eat and be satisfied."

> For he will deliver the needy when he cries for help,
> The afflicted also, and him who has no helper.
> He will have compassion on the poor and needy,
> And the lives of the needy he will save.
> He will rescue their life from oppression and violence,
> And their blood will be precious in his sight. (Ps. 72:12–14)

CLAUDE AND PATRICIA ARE LIVING, UNFOLDING STORIES OF DELIVERANCE AND RESTORATION

In the lives of Claude and Patricia, God was ordaining temporary affliction to accomplish a myriad of redemptive purposes in their lives. Affliction gave them a meager sampling of even grosser pains that they should have received in this life and the next (Mark 9:47–49). It alerted them to human sinfulness, including their own. It alerted them to their need for a Savior. And God provided them with a Savior in Jesus Christ. Now God was using their hardships as a means for them to know and appreciate Christ more deeply (Phil. 3:7–11).

Suffering offered a taste of Christ's afflictions to aid their devotion to him and worship of him (Acts 5:41–42). Suffering offered a constant motivation for them to long for Christ's appearing (2 Tim. 4:7–8). They were being forced to look heavenward and think eternally because their earthly trials provided a stark and vivid contrast to the glories of eternal life that they were soon to enjoy in his presence forever (Rom. 8:18).

Once Claude and Patricia began to see and seize their hardships from this point of view, their hearts were primed to worship God with greater sincerity and zeal. They were ready to sing his praises. They were ready to **stand in awe of him and worship him**, a God so wise and mighty, a God so able to use unspeakable and perplexing pain in their lives to bring about such a marvelous end.

The very fact that God ordained abuse as a means to draw them nearer to himself and help them appreciate Jesus more fully; the reality that God could redeem abuse in such a way for them to know him more deeply; the possibility that their sufferings set the stage for him to deliver at the proper time—all these truths and many more simply compelled their hearts to love and worship Jesus Christ. Not every incident of abuse might draw us to these conclusions, but Clause and Patricia came to believe that the gospel helped them to make sense of their experiences. And it motivated them to heartfelt worship.

The Spirit of God used the gospel to redefine Claude and Patricia's entire view of God, themselves, abuse, and just about everything else. It was not a fix-all, but a massive paradigm shift. It didn't change their past and present experiences, but it helped them to make better sense of them. It didn't take away all their pain, but it helped them to see the glory of God's grace shining through and using their pain.

> All the ends of the earth will remember and turn to the LORD,
> And all the families of the nations will worship before You.
> For the kingdom is the LORD's
> And He rules over the nations.
> All the prosperous of the earth will eat and worship,
> All those who go down to the dust will bow before Him,
> Even he who cannot keep his soul alive.
> Posterity will serve Him;
> It will be told of the Lord to the coming generation.
> They will come and will declare His righteousness
> To a people who will be born, that He has performed it.
>   (Ps. 22:27–31)

These verses were icing on the cake for Claude and Patricia. The words brought everything they were thinking and feeling to the proper conclusion: prayer for the whole world and every generation to know and worship their great God. In these words God seemed bigger to them than ever before. People and problems seemed to shrink.

The universe should come and bow, for God owns and governs and rules all he has made. He judges with justice. He saves by grace. He "causes all things to work together for good to those who love God, to those who are called according to His purpose" (Rom. 8:28). This assurance solidified Claude and Patricia's desire to go and declare to as many people as the Lord allowed the marvels and wonders and mercies of their Redeemer.

Of course, this one meeting and psalm didn't fix everything in Claude and Patricia's life. It wasn't supposed to. Life and marriage continued to bring daily challenges and hourly struggles. Their life and marriage trajectory, however, was being drastically changed. The perspectives and attitudes of their hearts were being transformed by the grace of God. The Spirit of God used Psalm 22 to give them comfort, hope, and strength in ways they couldn't imagine. They could see Christ in the middle of their lives. They had a better sense of what he was doing with them. They could begin to see the love of God being poured upon their marriage. They could begin to see their pride and selfishness with more clarity. They started repenting with more sincerity.

The road that Claude and Patricia are now walking includes much more of Jesus Christ. It moves toward God rather than away from him. Whenever painful memories and "old wounds" invade their conversations and interactions, they can reflect on the wise truth and convicting comforts of Psalm 22. In fact, they began finding similar wisdom and comfort throughout the Scriptures as a whole. Christ has become more real to them on every page. They can see how the Word speaks to all of life, not just abuse and marital conflict. So great is the love, wisdom, and power of our God!

A FEW WORDS AND QUESTIONS FOR PERSONAL APPLICATION

Though Psalm 22 can comfort and convict us in many forms under many circumstances, eight particular steps emerged for Claude and Patricia and proved helpful to them during the days after they were exposed to this truth of Scripture. Whenever they felt the weight of suffering and abuse, they tried to remember these truths and postures. It might be a good time for you to consider them, too. In fact, it might be helpful to consider a few areas of personal pain and struggle in your life right now and how you might take these truths and comforts to your own soul.

1. *Face God.* Talk to him! (Ps. 22:1–2). Be humble and be honest about what is going on in your heart. Be candid about how you see and respond to the Lord.

   • When mistreated, crushed, or wronged, do you run toward God or away from him? Do you seek him or avoid him?
   • At those moments when you are most confused, do you cry out to God for help? Do you fix your eyes on Jesus? Do you open up to him, or shut down?

2. *Trust God*, and his faithfulness from ages past (vv. 3–5). We are not alone, but have joined a legion of saints who trusted God under brutal circumstances.

   • When things go bad, do you see God as friend or foe, good or evil, a helper or an adversary?
   • Are you prone to look upon God with suspicion? Is Jesus a Savior or a threat to your soul? Do you bank on his promises or doubt them?

3. *Face reality*, and your experiences of humiliation, disgrace, and mocking (vv. 6–8).

- Are you learning to face adversity head-on with the strength that the Spirit provides? Or do you prefer to live in denial—minimizing and excusing your hardships and sins, and pretending that they will just go away on their own?
- Do you talk to God in honest ways? Do you share the truth with good friends and counselors? Do other people really know what's going on inside you?

4. ***Know to whom you belong***, and always have (vv. 9–10). Only God has a legitimate claim to our souls and lives.

- Are you able to see yourself as God's precious child? Do you believe that you are his possession?
- Does pain tempt you to question whether you are his eternal child? Are you secure or insecure? Do you feel and act like a beloved child or an unwanted orphan?

5. ***Face your weakness and desperation***, as prey before predator, as suffering at the hands of evildoers (vv. 11–15). The reality of our weakness should not drive us to greater self-sufficiency or rage, but to humble dependence on the Lord.

- What are you doing with your frailty? Do you hide it or gladly confess it? Do you veil it in toughness and anger or embrace it in the hands of your heavenly Father?
- Whom do you rely on when things crumble? Whom do you hope in? Are you still trying to convince yourself that you can figure it out and pull it together on your own, or are you coming to see your every-moment desperate need for grace?

6. ***Behold Christ amid your affliction.*** You have fellowship in his sufferings. Consider him. Our salvation cost him far more than it costs us (vv. 16–18).

- When you suffer, do you fix your eyes on Jesus Christ (with the strength that his Spirit supplies), or do you fix them more firmly on yourself?
- Have you come to appreciate the cross of Christ more deeply? How might the hardships you endure help you to consider the affliction that Christ endured on your behalf with more gratitude?

7. ***Remember that deliverance is certain and to God*** (vv. 19–21, 26–29). The promise of deliverance from pain and hardship will be fulfilled in the next life, but not yet. The Lord always delivers at the proper time.

- Is Jesus Christ the treasure of your soul? Are you willing to lose everything else in order to gain him?
- Are you coming to see deliverance in this life as deliverance *to God* rather than deliverance to easy life?
- On whom or on what have you fixed your hope? Are you coming to bank on the absolutely certain deliverance of God at the proper time?

8. ***Stand in awe of him and worship him*** (vv. 25–26, 30–31). As awkward and strange as it may sound, suffering provides a beautiful stage for pure-hearted worship. The gospel helps us to see what God is doing on a cosmic, eternal level, helping us to look upward in praise rather than cave inward on ourselves in self-absorbed pity and despair.

- Does pain compel you to worship or to complain? Do you hit your knees or raise your fist?
- When you survey your past, are you in awe of God's power and patience toward you? Are you amazed at how he has authored and continues to author your life?